I0158301

INNER THOUGHTS

A poetic journey from childhood to adulthood

DWIGHT A. DICKERSON

"Inner Thoughts" is a collection of poems and inspirational insights that I have compiled from childhood through adulthood expressing my inner thoughts about life, love, wisdom, hope, failures, family and spiritual consciousness.

Copyright © 2012 Dwight Dickerson
All rights reserved.

DEDICATION

This book is dedicated to my mother Dora Dickerson, who has since went home to be with the Lord. "Inner Thoughts" is the offspring of her encouragement, love and support which enabled me to express myself through writing.
Thanks mom.

CONTENTS

SECTION 1

"AGE OF INNONCENCE"

Poems written from the eyes of a child
(Ages 7-12)

Changing World

Is it me?

I do not know,

can it be?

I do not know.

Things are changing,

can I be too?

I do not know.

Can this be true?

I look around,

wondering why?

Things are changing,

in front of my eyes.

Forms are changing,

can I be too?

Please tell me,

can this be true?

(Penned at the age of 9)

Loneliness

There's a want within my heart,

and tears within my eyes.

But no-one hears and no –one cares

O Lord, I wonder why?

Though I yell out with pain,

and in so much sorrow.

No one hears and no one cares,

and for me there is no tomorrow.

Friends I don't have, there's no helping hand,

I cry out night and day on this forsaken land.

Trouble and scared I am-you see,

for loneliness can be explained by looking at me.

For there's a want within my heart and tears within my

eyes,

yet no one hears and no one cares O Lord I wonder

why?

As I yell out in pain and with so much sorrow,

no one hears and no one cares for me there is no

tomorrow.

(Penned at the age of 11)

Mom and Dad

Dear mom and dad I have to say,

I met this girl on my way.

she's so sweet, she's really neat,

she's so nice and so meek.

She followed me home for quite a while,

maybe one or two miles.

She so lovely and so fine,

I believe she's one of a kind.

Dear mom and dad can I keep her?

just a while so you can see her.

gee she's so cute and so fine,

she'll blow your mind.

Please mom and dad can she stay?"

I promise I'll watch her every day.

even during the time we sleep and play,

please mom and dad can she stay?

O thank you very much,

I really love her such.

I thank God for you today,

here girl, you can stay!

(Penned at the age of 7)

Question and Answer

What can you write when you fell like writing and have

nothing to

say?

What can be swirling in your mind, yet you cannot put

it on paper?

You feel you have to write something, but what?

This question comes up and is very hard to answer.

You may think of a lot of topics, but either they're too

dull

or the topic has already been exhausted by you.

At this moment I'm in this situation,

can't think of anything to write or say.

But sooner or later something

will come to your mind.

This did.

(Penned at the age of 9)

Reality

This is reality
that is that
white is white
black is black.

Sky may be blue,
grass may be green.
You may be you,
and I may be me.

You may snicker, you may sneer,
you can do anything, I don't care.
You may tremble in your fear,
but reality is right here.

Some may tremble,
some may run.
But when the day is done,
Reality will have won.
(Penned at the age of 10)

The Home I Once Wanted

The home I once wanted was so happy and gay
it seemed like the people in it felt the same way.
They smiled and smiled all day long
even when the day was gone.

The house stood bold and tall
and dared anything to try to make her fall.
The sun showed bright
and engulfed the house with light

So everyone could see
How happy the house made me.
Then one day, mother passed away
and the house I once wanted was gone.

Everyone was sad
even our dog Glad.
And the happiness was no more to be had

There I was with a broken heart,

I thought the house would never fall apart.

But death came in and sat right down

turning my home upside down.

(Penned at the age of 11)

The Star

The star has a special light

that shines both far and near.

The light that is so very bright

and shines throughout the years.

The beauty that it show us still

we can't sometimes bear.

Shining against our will at night

we know it will always be there.

The star was the guiding light

that helped the wise men find.

The baby in the manger

who came to save mankind.

It shows it light for all to see

the beauty it has to share.

At night we can bet it will be

shining with light to spare.

(Penned at the age of 8)

There Has To Be

There has to be a star for me somewhere afar,

shining for me radiating my destiny.

Somewhere afar there has to be my road,

a long winding road never ending, always fulfilling with

every step I

take.

All I want to be is someone someday,

there has to be my star, shining afar.

And as every step I make growing stronger,

I will not hesitate to let the world know I am here!

My star is awaiting and one day I shall be taking,

It's long winding and overdue glory.

(Penned at the age of 8)

What Can I Make?

Sitting here doodling with nothing on my mind,
sitting here doodling with nothing but time.

Time to waste, time to spare,
time to think, time to care

Sitting here doodling just being bored,

Watching the clock, knowing soon I'll be out the door.

But how time moves so slowly, yet I'll have to wait,

in the meantime, let me see what else I can make.
(Penned at the age of 10)

SECTION 2

"ADOLENCENT TO ADULTHOOD"
(13 to Adulthood)

A Christian Love Affair

I never knew that I could feel
Love within me so strong, so real.
I never knew the joy I could share with someone
In a Christian love affair.

Worldly desires don't stand a chance,
There's no room in a Christian romance.
Only true love from the Lord we love,
Who guides our every step from above.

I never knew I could feel this way,
Yet it gets better day after day.

And as I live I vow to share
with you and only you, my dear
"A Christian Love Affair"
(Our wedding poem)

Born Into This World

Gentle as a fresh summer's day,
Glistening in the warmth of the sun rays.
Standing tall, swaying to the gentle breeze,
Sweet as a new born baby as sweet as one could be.

Born into this world with happiness and love to share,
Born into this world with the showing that you care.
As your mystical light shines bright and true,
The world should stop and thank the Lord for you.

And in the stillness of the whispering wind,
Echoes your beauty again and again.
And as your beauty pierces through all our hearts,
Leaving a lasting image that shall never depart.

Born into this world with happiness and love to share,
Born into this world with the showing that you care.
As your mystical light shines bright and true,
The world should stop and thank the Lord for you.

For I Need No Special Day

My love, though today is a special day in the lives of
many,
for every day is special in my life knowing I have you.
Because I do not need a special day to tell you how
much I care,
Or to express all of my love for you.

For every day is a special day in my life,
knowing that there is that special someone in my life
giving me joy
and happiness.
For I need no special day to say thank you my love,
and I need no special day to show the world how much
you mean to
me.

Just like the sun, I too rise every day in the warmth of
your love,
and like a rose, I too grow and blossom in the beauty of
you.
For every day is a special day in my life,

for I need no special day to say I love you.

So my love, as the world celebrates this day,

I celebrate every day, every hour and every minute.

For I need no special day to show you how much I

care,

for I need no special day to say I love you.

My love.
(A valentine poem for my wife)

Hopelessly &Helplessly

Dedicated to my lovely wife Loretta for being the
woman that she is.

Hopelessly in love with you

helplessly I am.

I've tried to hide my love for you

but hopelessly I can't.

Hopelessly in debt to you

helplessly I trust.

My life, my love my everything

hopelessly I must.

Hopelessly I see myself
Helplessly I do.
Engaging in beautiful thoughts
hopelessly of you.

Hopelessly I find myself
helplessly in tears.
Wanting to hold you close to me
hopelessly wishing you was here.

Hopelessly I stumble around
helplessly in a daze.
Not knowing what's up or down
helplessly insane.

But one thing I do know my dear
just as the days do change.
I enjoy being hopelessly in love with you,
and helplessly I shall remain.

I Finally Found My Answer

There are times in our lives we find ourselves with
outstretched hands
reaching for that understanding, which in someone or
something we one day hope to find.
And within the joys and happiness which we will share
with one another while on this land.
our wants and desires shall one day be answered in
time.

In someone we can find ourselves in such
joys and sorrows
that we care not and want not for tomorrow.
For life's meanings and life's encounters have different
meaning and understanding which are new.
So my love, I can say with my outstretched hands, in
search for truth and understanding
I found you.

For my cares are diverted to you as my life is changed,
my true values of life have been rearranged.

I care not what happens tomorrow, for your love can
pull me through, for I thank the Lord for you.
As the starlight shine in the mist of darkness I too
shine, and with the power of your love I find my
destiny.

No longer do I find my life troubled or confused with
the pains of today's time.

For I only see the future, living with you, in love, for
you are my true destiny.
And as we live, let us grow together for we are the
foundation, the beginning of a new life, a new love,
with a new meaning.
I finally found my answer.

Inner Thoughts of a Black Man

Confused of the present, uncertain and scared,
scared of the future, uncertain of its encounters.
Memories of life,
and living with the uncertainty of tomorrow.
Past, present and future,

happy, uncertain, scared.

So what will my time be controlled by,
and how shall I control time?

Remembering the sad memories of the toils and fears
of yesterday,
unable to cope with the troubles of today,
Is it wrong to relive yesterday?

Yesterday's understanding,
yesterday's happiness.
Yesterday's love
yesterday's courage.

As my heart yearns for comfort,
yesterday turns into today and today leads tomorrow by
the hand.
Fears, confusion, unhappiness, hate is side by side,
to relive yesterday's love for tomorrows fault, is our
decision.

And as the future holds our time
Is it wrong to relive Yesterday?

Is It Worth It?

Is it worth it for one to give
to this world in which we live,.
One's tears, one's life to be,
a beacon of light in this society.

To continue on carving out new trails,
knowing the hardship and pain entailed.
Accepting the fight one will have to face,
to make this world a better place.
Is It Worth It?

Let Me

Let me touch you with just my smile, to let you know I
care,
let me love you for a while so together our hearts can
share.

The joys and sorrows of tomorrow with every step we take,
the ups and downs to be found within the vows we shall make.

Let me show you with my eyes how I really feel,
let me hold you within my arms so you'll know I'm real.
For I don't doubt, I know without, hesitation or worry,
our love is above all, the greatest love story.

Not Enough Days

There are 365 days in a year, and I still find it hard my dear,
to thank you for the wonderful things you do
even to let you know how much I care for you.

Even when leap year comes around
and there's an extra day to be found
I still can't find the time on hand
to thank you enough for being my friend.

For sharing a smile when there was a need,
and for being the person you ought to be.

I wish I had the power to change the hours
the minutes I would rearrange so that time
would go on without being subjected to days.
Then and only then, will I find the time to say.

How much I love you, how much I care,
how much I appreciate you being here.
How wonderful you are, and I'm glad to be,
the one you choose for eternity.

Remember?

The shrilling cries of yesterday's sorrow, yesterday pain,
which were heard by many but understood by just a
few.
The ugliness that was for millions their only true vision
their only true world, beauty had no meaning.
Remember?

The loneliness, the confusions, the illusions, the
darkness,
for tomorrow had no meaning, no real reason for
belonging.
Light, there was none, hope was not theirs to
encounter,
lost, confused, frighten, unable to live and blissful to
die.
Remember?

Their plight, their ancestor's plight and their struggle
for life,
wars fought, land fertilized, cities molded from bare
hands,
seen by many, but understood by just a few.
Remember?

The past wars for freedom, peace and equality,
the wars for unity, among those for belief.
Our pride and cultural heritage fought for by many
to be understood and respected.
Remember?

Yesterday's sorrows, and today's joy,

yesterday's wars and today's tranquility.

Yesterday's forefathers, as well as today's and

tomorrow's,

we now feel what they believed in.

Remember?

We live in the reflections of their failures and their

accomplishments.

Their cries became the seed of our existence as well as

our joys.

For we have strength and hope when at one time there

was none.

For our tomorrows now have meaning when once

there was none.

Remember

Separate Corners

Sweetheart, though we sit in different corners separated

by land and

time

looking at our different horizons through different

color windows

thinking the same thoughts of love

seeing the same beautiful visions

of joy while feeling the same excitement

understanding with each minute that goes by, brings us

once more

together.

Though, in the darkest times in my corner there kindles

a light

reflecting my thoughts of you

and as I welcome each new horizon, each new day, I

too welcome

them for you.

In my coldest times in my corner

the warmth of your love encapsulates me.

And in the hottest times in my corner
the coolness of your breath keeps me
in its full cooling winds.

In my times of uneasiness in my corner
the soothing vibrations of our lullaby of love
places me once again at ease.
I find in my time of wants, in you I have everything.
For I want not much from this world but to be content
and in my corner, captured in thoughts
of our love I find contentment.

Yet my love, there is such a yearning within my heart
wishing and wanting to be within your touch.

There is no other time when I feel, secure as I do when
find myself
locked between your arms, locked in place by love,
beauty and
understanding.

For I find it is at this time that I care not
if tomorrow would come just as long as I can spend
each precious moment with you.

So, as we both sit in our separate corners
separated by land and time, watching out different
horizons
yet thinking the same thoughts of love.
Let us find each other through the love we share,
comfort and sooth our most empty feelings of
loneliness.

For we are together in heart, soul and mind, which
miles and time
cannot change
even though our corners may be separated by land and
time.
And as the days come and go, my love
I find myself closer to you today more than
Yesterday.

The Simple Things in Life

Walk with me along the beach; we'll count the grains of
sand,
or build sandcastles three feet high and spend some
times as friends.

The simple things in life I find brings the greatest
amount of joy,
especially when we share them with that special girl or
boy.

I pray that we can find that joy in the simple things we
do,
as we share from day to day, throughout our whole life
through.

I find myself more each day waiting to share with you,
all the simple things in life forever and a day plus two.

You Are the Reason

I awake each new morning
with great joy as it starts.
With a song on my lips,
that flows right from my heart.

I sing because I'm happy
a joyful melody.

I sing because I'm happy,
that you're a part of me.

I find myself each morning,
taking time out to pray.
Thanking my heavenly Father,
for giving me this day.

To share it with an angel,
of such beauty and grace.
With a heart like an ocean
that no one can replace.

I sing because I'm happy,
a joyful melody.
I sing because that angel,
chose to share her life with me.

You're the reason why I sing
my joyful melody.
A song that I will always sing,
as long as you're with me.

SECTION 3

"ILLUMINATIONS"

A series of inspirational insights to live by.

"ACCEPTANCE"

I searched upon the mountaintops

And found you were not there

So I searched the valleys below

I searched the deserts, the cities,

And pastures of green

Longing to find you so

I searched amongst the stars above

And found you were not there

So I searched the seven seas

Then I searched within my heart

And found you inside

Me.

"A DAILY PRAYER"

Give me strength O Lord I pray

Help me through these trying days.

To run this race which you've laid out,

And live for you apart from doubt.

Strengthen my heart O Lord I pray,

So I can love as you say

And show to all who don't believe,

The wondrous works you've done in me.

"Pray at all times, on every occasion,
In every season; in Spirit with all manner of
Prayer and entreaty"
(Ephesians 6:18)

"A FATHER'S LOVE"

My love is a love not swayed by your height,

Nor your weight nor by the complexion of your

skin.

<u>My love is unconditional!</u>

Reaching far beyond your failures and your

accomplishments,

Penetrating through to the marrow of your bones.

<u>My Love is unconditional!</u>

Never ending, always accepting and always

giving,

My love is a love that money can't

buy and time can't erase.

<u>My love is everlasting!</u>

For nothing can separate you from my

love.

<u>"I'm Your Father"</u>

"BE MINDFUL"

The words we speak

Can change lives for a moment,

But the examples we leave

Can change them

For a life time.

So let us be mindful

Not only of what we say,

But most importantly,

WHAT WE DO!

"For this you have been called, because Christ also suffered for
you, leaving you an example that you should follow in his
steps." (I Peter 3:21)

"EVEN THE MOUNTAINS"

Even the mountains in all

their splendor,

Great trophies in God's

precious sky

Can never in a million years

surpass the beauty you posses

inside.

"FIRM FOUNDATION"

O how foolish can one be
To think a house would stand,
When the house is built
Upon a foundation
Made of sand

For when the winds and water comes
the house will be washed away,
For a wise man builds his house
upon the foundation
Christ has laid.

*"For no other foundation can anyone lay than that which
already laid, which is Jesus Christ,
the Messiah, the Anointed one"*
(1Corinthians 3:11)

"God's Handiwork"

When I see God's handy work

I find it hard to believe

Out of all of His mighty works

He gave his best to me.

"HATE"

Hate is liken unto a

Tornado

Once aground

Destroys everything in its

Path!!

"HEAVEN"

Heaven is liken unto a

Rainbow

For in order to experience the

Beauty of either one

You must first weather the

Storm!

"LOVE"

*Love is liken unto the
sun,*

*For both shed light
onto a darken
World....*

"LOVE ABOUND"

It's when we put aside our differences

and allow ourselves to open up

our hearts to the needs of

others,

Then and only then will true

love abound.

"Love bears all things, believes all things, Hopes all things, and
endures all things Love never fails". (1 Corinthians
13:7-8)

"NO GREATER SOUND NO GREATER JOY"

There's no greater sound than

the laughter of children,

There's no greater joy than being the

source of their

laughter!

"SOMEONE'S AT THE DOOR"

I stand in the door and knock.

Compassionately,

I knock

Gentlemanly,

I knock

Patiently,

I knock

I wait

For you to

Open

*"Behold, I stand at the door and knock: If any man
hears my voice
and open the door, I will come in to him and will sup
with him and
him with me. (Revelations 3:20)*

"THOU STANDETH ALONE"

Since the beginning,

Thou reigneth supreme,

You've showed me how great

Thou Art.

Surely Thou standeth alone

O God,

In heaven and in my

Heart

"YOUR LOVING KINDNESS"

Your loving kindness is

immeasurable,

Stretching across both

land and sea.

Changing lives of so many O Lord,

As it did for a sinner

like me.

"God commends His love toward us, in that while we

were yet

sinners.

Christ died for us". (Romans 5:8)

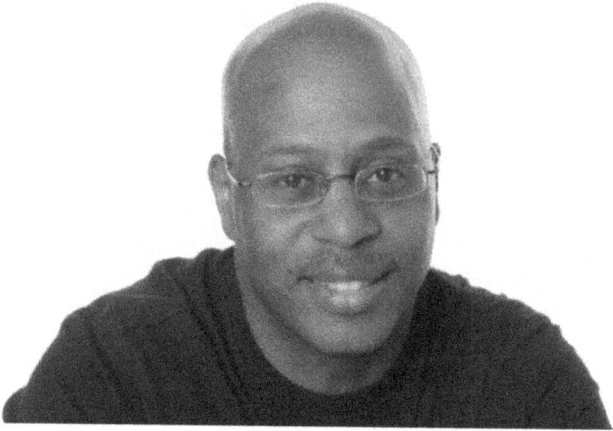

Poet, composer and musician,

Born and raised in the Bronx to the parents of Elmore and Dora Dickerson, Dwight has been writing poetry and composing music since the age of 7. Dwight is an accomplished musician receiving his training from Yale University in New Haven, CT., Berklee College of Music in Boston, Ma. and Howard University in Washington, D. C.

Dwight holds a MA in Community Psychology from the University of New Haven and a BA in Sociology from Yale University. When Dwight is not writing, playing or composing music, he takes on the role as a Community Psychologist and President / CEO of Tri-Cord LLC New Haven, an "Empowerment Training Group" dedicated to empowering individuals with the tools to be successful.

www.ingramcontent.com/pod-product-compliance
Lightning Source LLC
Chambersburg PA
CBHW021920040426
42448CB00007B/835